Famine and Fortune

Ruth

by Barry Webb
&
David Höhne

Famine and Fortune
© Matthias Media 1996

Matthias Media
(St Matthias Press Ltd ACN 067 558 365)
PO Box 225
Kingsford NSW 2032
Australia
Telephone: (02) 9663 1478; international: +61-2-9663-1478
Facsimile: (02) 9663 3265; international: +61-2-9663-3265
Email: info@matthiasmedia.com.au
Internet: www.matthiasmedia.com.au

Matthias Media (USA)
Telephone: 724 964 8152; international: +1-724-964-8152
Facsimile: 724 964 8166; international: +1-724-964-8166
Email: sales@matthiasmedia.com
Internet: www.matthiasmedia.com

ISBN 978 1 875245 55 0

Cover design and typesetting by Lankshear Design Pty Ltd.

Contents

How to make the most of these studies 5

1 Going away and coming back (Ruth 1:1-22)..........9

2 The kindness of God (Ruth 2:1-23) 17

3 Encounter on the threshing floor (Ruth 3:1-18)....25

4 The redeemer (Ruth 4:1-22) 31

Tips for leaders 39

How to make the most of these studies

1. What is an Interactive Bible Study?

These 'interactive' Bible studies are a bit like a guided tour of a famous city. The studies will take you through Ruth, pointing out things along the way, filling in background details, and suggesting avenues for further exploration. But there is also time for you to do some sightseeing of your own—to wander off, have a good look for yourself, and form your own conclusions.

In other words, we have designed these studies to fall halfway between a sermon and a set of unadorned Bible study questions. We want to provide stimulation and input and point you in the right direction, while leaving you to do a lot of the exploration and discovery yourself.

We hope that these studies will stimulate lots of 'interaction'—interaction with the Bible, with the things we've written, with your own current thoughts and attitudes, with other people as you discuss them, and with God as you talk to him about it all.

2. The format

Each study contains sections of text to introduce, summarize, suggest and provoke. We've left plenty of room in the margins for you to jot comments and questions as you read.

Interspersed throughout the text are two types of 'interaction', each with their own symbol:

Investigate

Questions to help you investigate key parts of the Bible.

Think it through

Questions to help you think through the implications of your discoveries and write down your own thoughts and reactions.

When you come to one of these symbols, you'll know that it's time to do some work of your own.

3. Suggestions for individual study

- Before you begin, pray that God would open your eyes to what he is saying in Ruth and give you the spiritual strength to do something about it. You may be spurred to pray again at the end of the study.
- Work through the study, following the directions as you go. Write in the spaces provided.
- Resist the temptation to skip over the *Think it through* sections. It is important to think about the sections of text (rather than just accepting them as true) and to ponder the implications for your life. Writing these things down is a very valuable way to get your thoughts working.
- Take what opportunities you can to talk to others about what you've learnt.

4. Suggestions for group study

- Much of the above applies to group study as well. The studies are suitable for structured Bible study or cell groups, as well as for more informal pairs and threesomes. Get together with a friend/s and work through them at your own pace; use them as the basis for regular Bible study with your spouse. You don't need the formal structure of a 'group' to gain maximum benefit.

- It is *vital* that group members work through the study themselves *before* the group meets. The group discussion can take place comfortably in an hour (depending on how side-tracked you get!), but only if all the members have done the work and are familiar with the material.
- Spend most of the group time discussing the 'interactive' sections—*Investigate* and *Think it through*. Reading all the text together will take too long and should be unnecessary if the group members have done their preparation. You may wish to underline and read aloud particular paragraphs or sections of text that you think are important.
- The role of the group leader is to direct the course of the discussion and to try to draw the threads together at the end. This will mean a little extra preparation—underlining important sections of text to emphasize, working out which questions are worth concentrating on, and being sure of the main thrust of the study. Leaders will also probably want to work out approximately how long they'd like to spend on each part.
- We haven't included an 'answer guide' to the questions in the studies. This is a deliberate move. We want to give you a guided tour of Ruth, not a lecture. There is more than enough in the text we have written and the questions we have asked to point you in what we think is the right direction. The rest is up to you.
- For more input see 'Tips for leaders' on page 39.

Before you begin

We recommend that before you start on study 1, you take the time to read right through Ruth in one sitting. This will give you a feel for the direction and purpose of the whole book and help you greatly in looking at each passage in its context.

Going away and coming back

In the Book of Ruth, we read one of the great love stories of the Bible. Boaz the rich and influential Israelite, and Ruth the poor but virtuous Moabite widow—so much seems to conspire to keep them apart, and yet in God's purposes they come together, and play an important part in the history of the whole nation (as we shall see).

In fact, much of the significance of the book of Ruth lies in its context; that is, in what takes place before and after it. As the very first verse tells us, the story is set "in the days when the judges ruled". In this period (which is described in the book of Judges), Israel had no king and no formal centralised administration. She depended upon specially gifted men and women that God raised up to provide leadership. They were called 'judges' because they carried out God's judgment, either by driving out enemies or by settling disputes among the Israelites themselves.

In practice, however, the system (if that is the correct term for it) rarely worked smoothly. There was very little unity among the Israelite tribes in the period of the Judges.

For a start, they were separated from each other by settlements of unconquered Canaanites (Judg 1:19, 27-36; 4:2-3). Unlike the Israelites, these people had farmed the land for generations, and attributed their success at raising crops to their worship of the various male and female nature gods, the Baals and the Ashtoreths. They believed that these 'gods' controlled the land and the weather, and hence the fertility of field and flock.

The Israelites were very attracted to these gods and increasingly mixed the worship of them with the worship of their own God, Yahweh. This inevitably led to a weakening of their loyalty to God and to one another, and resulted in spiritual and moral decline that was so serious it threatened to destroy Israel from within. The tribes were slow to help each other in times of crisis, and even fell to fighting among themselves (Judg 5:16-17, 8:1-3, 12:1-6). Most people were concerned only for their own interests and took advantage of the absence of central government to do as they pleased (Judg 17:6, 21:25). This inner decay threatened to destroy the very fabric of Israel and in fact constituted a far more serious threat to its survival in the Judges period than any external attack.

The book of Judges could be summarised as a cycle of Israel's sin, God's judgment of them at the hands of an enemy, Israel's repentance and call for help, and the raising up of a saviour-judge who rescued Israel from the enemy (e.g. Samson, Gideon or Ehud). It is within this chaotic cycle that we read the story of Naomi, Ruth and Boaz. In it, we see how God very quietly goes about the business of saving Israel from her enemies and from herself, and unfolding his plan for the salvation of the world.

We will come back to these big themes, especially when we reach chapter 4, but first let us begin where Ruth begins, with leaving home.

Going away

Ruth chapter 1 is a story about going away and coming back. In the Bible there are many such stories. Abraham went down to Egypt because of a famine, and later returned. The whole family of Israel went down to Egypt, again because of a famine, and later was brought back to their land by God in the Exodus. Later in her history, Israel went into exile and then returned. Jesus told the famous story of the Prodigal son who went away but came back. In fact the whole Bible is the story of mankind leaving paradise and returning.

The opening verses of Ruth, then, with their description of people leaving the land because of famine, alert us straight away that something is in the wind. Something significant is going to happen. It's the old pattern of God working some act of salvation when his people leave their land.

Investigate

Read Ruth 1:1-7.

1. Why do Elimelech and his family leave the land?

2. Why is Moab a rather odd place to go (compare Deut 23:3-6; Judg 3:12-15, 26-30)?

3. What did Elimelech and his family gain by going to Moab (in the short term and the long term)?

4. Why does Naomi come back?

In Ruth 1:6 we read that the Lord had come to the aid of his people (in their time of need) and given them food. At this point in the story we are reminded of the grace, goodness and kindness of God towards Israel during the period of the Judges (Judg 3:11). We see that God acts for his people and we note that Naomi returns because of what God has done.

The journey home (1:8-22)

Naomi resolutely sets out for Judah, accompanied by her two daughters-in-law, Orpah and Ruth. What draws them after Naomi? Is it simply the bond that has grown between them, or the abundance of food now to be had in Israel? Or is it perhaps that their remarriage prospects will be better there? After all, their first husbands had been Israelites. But Naomi regards their prospects of remarriage in Israel as nil, and for this reason urges them to leave her and return to their own land and people (vv. 8-14).

Finding a husband may have been possible in Moab, but Naomi can see no chance of it in Israel. She herself would have to provide them with husbands again. But this is an impossibility, given her age. Orpah recognises the logic of the situation and tearfully takes her leave; Naomi has correctly read Orpah's motivation for following her to Israel.

But with Ruth it is otherwise. She vows to stay with Naomi, come what may, and even to embrace Naomi's God. Keats, in his poem 'The Nightingale', describes Ruth as the heartsick daughter far away from home. However, we will see as the story continues to unfold that it is not Ruth who is sick at heart, but Naomi. Ruth comes in and shares in the blessings of God. Ironically, Naomi's understanding of God's goodness and grace seems less than Ruth's, who is a foreigner.

Investigate

Compare the speeches of Ruth (vv. 16-17) and Naomi (vv. 20-21).

1. Do they each see God as in control of events? How do they express this?

   • Ruth

   • Naomi

2. What is their attitude to this God, given all that has happened?

   • Ruth *God will be my God*

   • Naomi *Bitter*

3. How do they see the future?

- Ruth

  Hope

- Naomi

  β. Hermess – anger

Naomi's words in this scene are very revealing. She believes she has been severely disciplined by the Lord. She and her family had gone to Moab, to the land of the enemy, in search of food. They had left the land of God's blessing, and now she was returning without husband or sons—empty.

She regards the whole situation with bitterness and regret. Her life is in ruins, and she is in no doubt as to who has done this to her. Four times in her short speech she attributes her misfortune and affliction to the Almighty, to Yahweh the God of Israel.

Ruth, on the other hand, seems keen to align herself with this same God of Israel who has taken her husband from her. Her loyalty to Naomi, and her desire to submit to Naomi's God, is in stark contrast to Naomi's own bitterness and disillusionment.

This odd couple arrive back in Bethlehem, without husbands and without prospects. As we shall see, God has some surprises in store for them.

Think it through

1. Naomi is as full of bitterness as the Israelites were in Egypt before God redeemed them. She does not seem to expect much from God. Do you find yourself viewing God in this way?

2. Are there times when you feel like changing your name to 'bitter'? What is your attitude to God at these times?

3. What does this chapter tell us about how God works?

4. In what ways is Ruth's behaviour an example to us?

The kindness of God

Our last study finished with Naomi and Ruth returning to Bethlehem, with the barley season just beginning. We are left wondering: "How will these two widows who have nothing and no family fend for themselves?".

Before the narrator can proceed, he must introduce us to Boaz, who will be a principal actor in the rest of the story. Boaz does not make his entry in person until verse 4, but already in verse 1 we are told some very significant things about him. He is a kinsman of Elimelech and 'a man of wealth'. Enter the rich relative! Could this be the man of 'fullness' who will make up for Naomi's emptiness?

Investigate

Read Ruth 2:1-7.

1. What is the difference between the responses of Naomi and Ruth to their situation (see 1:19-2:7)?

2. What impression do we get of Ruth in this passage (cf. 1:16-17)?

3. In verse 1 we have already learnt something about Boaz. What other things do we learn about him as he makes his appearance in the story?

When Boaz makes his personal entry, he does so with Yahweh, the name of the Lord, on his lips (v. 4).[1] He blesses the reapers in Yahweh's name and they respond in kind. All quite conventional perhaps, but the fact that it is mentioned adds a further dimension to the portrait of Boaz. He is not just a wealthy man, with a field and servants to reap it, but a pious and true Israelite who honours Yahweh in his conversation and the conduct of his business. And if Boaz is a model of piety, Ruth is a model of responsibility and industry. She is poor, but she is no beggar or thief. She courteously asks for permission to glean, and when it is granted works all day (v. 7). She does this, we remember, not just to meet her own needs, but to provide for Naomi.

Boaz and Ruth are both ideal figures, and there is already a suggestion that divine providence is drawing them together (v. 3). But in love stories there are normally impediments which have to be overcome before union can take place, and in the words of the reapers we are reminded of one potentially serious impediment in this case: Ruth is a Moabitess (v. 6).

---

1 English translations of the Bible use small capitals ('the LORD') to indicate the personal name of God.

Encounter in the fields

Investigate

Look up the following laws for Israel regarding the harvest:
Leviticus 19:9-10; Deuteronomy 24:19-22 (see also Deut 10:17-19).

1. What do these passages tell us about God's attitude to the poor, widows and foreigners?

2. Why were the Israelites to be especially mindful of strangers in their midst?

Read Ruth 2:8-16.

3. In verse 10 it would seem that Ruth's hopes were answered (v. 2), but she is puzzled as to why Boaz would take any notice of her. How does Boaz answer her?

4. What indications are there in the passage that not everyone might treat Ruth so kindly?

5. How does Boaz's treatment of Ruth mirror Ruth's treatment of Naomi?

Boaz's inquiry back in verse 5—"Whose young woman is that?"— revealed nothing of his attitude towards Ruth. It was simply a request for information which was entirely understandable in the circumstances. However, his behaviour towards Ruth in verses 8-16 shows him adopting a particular stance towards her. He confirms the permission already given by the reapers for her to glean his field. He gives her access to drinking water and invites her to share the meal with himself and his servants, and our attention is pointedly drawn in verse 14 to the generous way in which he plies her with food. This may be nothing more than the law required, but there are indications that such behaviour could not be taken for granted in the Israel of those times.

Notice how Boaz has to instruct even his own servants repeatedly not to molest or reproach Ruth (vv. 9, 15-16). And what of his instruction to her to glean exclusively in his own field (v. 8)? Is it simply to protect her, or is he also desiring to attach Ruth to himself? Boaz's behaviour is all very proper and correct, but there are signs that, consciously or not, Boaz has become a suitor. He is so concerned for her welfare in these verses that we rightly suspect that something more than piety and duty have begun to motivate him, even if he may not fully recognise it at this stage.

A place in the family

Investigate

Read Ruth 2:17-23.

1. What did Ruth do after all her hard work?

2. What was Naomi's reaction to Ruth's news?

3. What new piece of information do we learn about Boaz?

As the story unfolds, we discover that Naomi knows Boaz, and remembers that he is one of their "kinsman-redeemers" (v. 20). The Hebrew term (*go'el*) which Naomi uses here, is more specific than 'relative'. Like the English expression 'next of kin', it refers to a particularly close blood-relative. Under Israelite law, a *go'el* had special responsibilities, as we shall see.

Behind the kindness of Boaz is the kindness of Yahweh. Naomi who thought of herself as under a divine curse now sees herself as the object of divine blessing. Yahweh has disciplined her but not forsaken her. She recognises the hand of God in the events of the day and urges Ruth (one can sense her excitement and expectancy) to continue her association with Boaz (v. 22). Notice that the instrument in Yahweh's hand is a man whose attitudes and behaviour are in marked contrast to those of his fellow Israelites.

Think it through

Read Psalm 36:5-10 and Psalm 91:1-4.

1. What do these passages tell us about God's character?

2. How is the character of the God of Israel reflected in:

   • the laws regarding foreigners and harvest?

   • the behaviour of Boaz, the godly Israelite, towards Ruth?

3. What does your behaviour say about the God that you believe in? What is your attitude to strangers and foreigners? What is your attitude towards non-Christians (cf. Titus 3:1-3)?

4. Do you expect goodness and blessing from God, "under whose wings you have come to take refuge"?

5. Boaz's kindness is the kindness of Yahweh. What are some of the ways that God has been kind to you?

Encounter on the threshing floor

In the last chapter we were introduced to Boaz, the rich relative. We saw how through this godly man the Lord continued to look after Naomi and Ruth by providing food for them (cf. 1:6). We saw that through the kindness of Boaz the unexpected kindness of the Lord has started to take effect. We also began to get hints of the growing relationship between Boaz and Ruth that will take up much of the remaining story.

Investigate

Quickly read over both chapters 2 and 3. What similarities do you notice between the events of the two chapters?

-
-
-
-
-

We have noted the similarities between the two chapters, but there are also significant differences.

The first thing we notice is the dramatic shift that has taken place in Naomi's state of mind and in her relationship with Ruth. Her earlier pessimism has entirely disappeared, and she is the one who now takes the initiative. This time Ruth is sent by Naomi. Her mission is to capture Boaz as her husband, and Naomi gives her precise instructions on how to go about it. As a foreigner Ruth is entirely dependent on Naomi for knowledge of correct etiquette in this most delicate operation. Ruth may not fully understand why Boaz is such a good marriage prospect (this turns on the technicalities of Israelite law and local custom as we shall see), but she has enough confidence in Naomi's judgment to agree to do exactly as she says (v. 5). Uncovering of the feet or legs (v. 4) was apparently a polite invitation to sex and hence to marriage.

With Ruth's movement to the threshing floor in verse 6, the second and central scene of this third chapter is opened. Her verbal undertaking to do exactly as Naomi told her is now translated into action. Ruth speaks only when she is spoken to (v. 9), and her words are carefully chosen.

The contrast at this point with the corresponding scene in chapter two is striking. Ruth no longer refers to her foreignness, nor to the fact that she is not one of Boaz's servants. She simply identifies herself as "Ruth your maidservant". There is a new intimacy being claimed here in word and action. Her tone is deferential, but she presses her claim pointedly by addressing Boaz as her *go'el*, which implies obligation on his part (v. 9). Precisely what she expects of him has already been expressed by her uncovering his legs; it is now made plainer by the request, "Spread the corner of your garment (literally 'your wing') over me".

In the previous chapter Boaz had blessed Ruth in the name of Yahweh, under whose wings she had come to take refuge (2:12). Now she is asking Boaz to translate his pious words into action by being the means by which that blessing would take place. She is asking him to be her protector by taking her as his wife.

A redeemer for Ruth?

In order to grasp what is going on in the story at this point we need to have a quick look at what the Law of Moses says about "kinsman-redeemers".

Investigate

Read Leviticus 25:23-25 and Deuteronomy 25:5-10.

1. What provisions did the Law make for Israelites who fell into debt? Why were these made?

2. What provisions did the Law make for the preservation of families? What purpose did this serve?

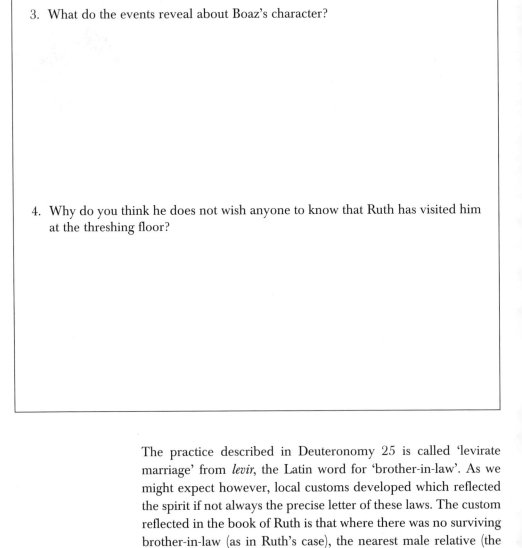

Now read Ruth 3:6-14.

3. What do the events reveal about Boaz's character?

4. Why do you think he does not wish anyone to know that Ruth has visited him at the threshing floor?

The practice described in Deuteronomy 25 is called 'levirate marriage' from *levir*, the Latin word for 'brother-in-law'. As we might expect however, local customs developed which reflected the spirit if not always the precise letter of these laws. The custom reflected in the book of Ruth is that where there was no surviving brother-in-law (as in Ruth's case), the nearest male relative (the *go'el*) was expected to fulfil both the property responsibility and the marriage responsibility. At this point in the story only marriage is on view. The property responsibility will become important in chapter 4.

In verse 11, Boaz declares his intention to marry Ruth, and the story seems set to move quickly to a happy conclusion. However, a bombshell is suddenly dropped into the happy scene; all this happy prospect is put into jeopardy by the disclosure that there is a nearer kinsman than Boaz (v. 12). One impediment—Ruth's foreignness—has been surmounted, but now a second and more formidable impediment appears. Someone else has prior title to Ruth, and given that Boaz's high estimation of her is probably shared by other men (v. 11), it seems that Boaz will have to give way. But Boaz, noble to the last, will not resort to malpractice to get Ruth; law and custom must have their way. The matter is out of the lovers' hands; they can only wait and see. But the mention of Yahweh in verse 13 is perhaps a subtle reminder that divine providence, not human whim, will be the final decider of issues in this story.

Think it through

Note the godly way that Boaz acts in this chapter. He is a rich and powerful man with a young woman offering herself for marriage. Ruth is a poor, alien widow. Boaz could easily have taken advantage of her. However, he remains resolute in his desire to keep the Law. He even puts his own happiness at risk by telling Ruth that there is another who has a better claim than himself (v. 12).

1. What contrast is there between the attitude and behaviour of Elimelech and Naomi in chapter 1, and Boaz in chapters 2 and 3?

2. In the story so far, how do both Boaz and Ruth show themselves willing to take shelter under God's wings? Is their trust well-placed?

3. Have you committed your cause to the Lord as both Ruth and Boaz did? When do you feel least like doing this?

The redeemer

Most movies that come out of Hollywood have a happy ending, the reason being that that's what people want to see. There's usually some tension, some doubt as to whether the hero will get the girl. But in the end we all feel much better when "they all live happily ever after".

It seems that the book of Ruth is no exception. The end of chapter 3 left us with considerable tension. Things seemed to be going smoothly between Ruth and Boaz until Boaz mentioned that someone else was in a better position to marry her. Will it all turn out right in the end?

The redeemer for Ruth

The setting for this final episode of the story, the town gate, has been subtly anticipated in Boaz's words in verse 11 of the previous chapter: "All my fellow townsmen (literally "all the gate of my people") know that you are a woman of noble character". The scene that now unfolds opens with another of those 'providential coincidences' with which the story is sprinkled, for who should happen to come by but the very man of whom Boaz has so recently spoken! Appropriate formalities are observed. Everything to be done will be duly witnessed and therefore legally binding. The authority with which Boaz acts in relation to the elders shows that he is indeed a man of importance in the community (cf. 2:1).

Investigate

Read Ruth 4:1-12.

1. Refer back to study 3. What provisions did the Law make for families and for Israelites who fell into debt?

2. What indications are there that Naomi is in poverty?

3. Why does the other 'kinsman-redeemer' give way to Boaz?

4. Rachel and Leah were Jacob's wives, the ancestral mothers of Israel. How is Ruth like them?

5. What connection does Rachel have with Bethlehem (see Gen 35:16-20)?

6. Read Genesis 38. What is similar about the story of Tamar and the story of Ruth? What does this tell us about the way God acts to achieve his purposes?

Now read Ruth 4:13-22.

7. How have the prayers of Naomi and Boaz been answered (cf. 1:9 and 2:12)?

8. How were the prayers of the elders and the women eventually answered through the offspring of Ruth and Boaz?

The redeemer for Israel

The story of Ruth begins with "in the days when the judges ruled" (1:1). It is against this backdrop that the events of Ruth need to be read. The Judges cycle—in which Israel repeatedly sinned, was judged, repented and was saved—was a period of 200 years of national chaos. In contrast to the unfaithfulness of Israel during this time, we see that very quietly God had been working out his plan to provide Israel with a redeemer in King David. The faithfulness and kindness of Ruth to Naomi, and Boaz to Ruth, was a small part of the continuing faithful kindness of Yahweh to an unfaithful Israel.

David was Yahweh's King, who brought Israel together for the first time since the days of Joshua. Under David, all Israel's enemies were subdued, her borders were extended, and there was rest in the land for God's people (2 Sam 7:8-11). The promises to Abraham were largely fulfilled, with the great throng of God's people living in the promised land, at rest from their enemies, and being a blessing to the nations around. We see a greater purpose to Ruth's story in the genealogy of David at the book's end.

The significance of the book of Ruth for the Old Testament people of God, then, was in showing the powerful kindness and grace of Yahweh. Despite their wanderings and unfaithfulness, he was absolutely constant in his plans. Even through the strange instrument of an impoverished Moabite widow, God would work to raise up the great king to lead his people to their golden age. God does it again—a story which starts with famine and leaving the land finishes with blessing and the continuation of the godly line that would lead to David—and beyond.

The book of Ruth is thus also a call to return to Yahweh, whose steadfast love is so in contrast to Israel's unfaithfulness. As we have noted previously, the book of Ruth begins with Naomi and her family going away from the Lord and his land. When she returned to Yahweh, empty and embittered, she was filled to overflowing with his blessing.

The redeemer for us

Matthew's Gospel begins with the genealogy of Jesus Christ, "the son of David, the son of Abraham". In the genealogy, only four women are mentioned, all of them unusual, and all of them connected with the book of Ruth. There is first of all Tamar, who gave birth to Perez by tricking her father-in-law Judah into sleeping with her (she is referred to in Ruth 4:12). Then there is Rahab, the faithful prostitute from Jericho, who happened to be the mother of Boaz. There is Ruth herself; and then Bathsheba, the adulteress who was the wife of David, the great king.

In Matthew, the significance of these four 'shady ladies' seems to be in showing how often God works in strange ways to achieve his purposes. When Jesus is born in somewhat controversial circumstances to a virgin in Bethlehem, we can see that it is actually nothing out of the ordinary. God is simply doing it again—working to redeem his people through an unlikely birth in Bethlehem, just as in the book of Ruth. This will culminate, of course, in that most unlikely of salvations—when Jesus is executed on a Roman cross, and in so doing saves the world.

We also see reflected in Ruth, and in the Gospels, the important truth that God is not only concerned with the nation of Israel—he is ultimately concerned to bring blessing to all the earth (as he originally promised to Abraham). Just as foreigners like Rahab, Ruth and Bathsheba play an important role in the genealogy of Jesus, so when we reach the end of Matthew's Gospel, the disciples of Jesus are commissioned to make disciples from every nation. In the end, even aliens and strangers (like most of us) can take shelter under the wings of Yahweh, the God of Israel.

Think it through

In many ways Ruth's story is our story (if we are Gentile Christians). Ruth was an alien. As a Gentile, she was not one of God's people and therefore separated from sharing in the blessings of a relationship with God. Yet in attaching herself to the God of Israel, she was provided with a redeemer.

Read Ephesians 2:11-22.

1. How is the story of Ruth similar to this?

2. If the book of Ruth records one stage in the unfolding of God's great plan, what was the end point towards which the whole plan was moving? (Answer from the Ephesians passage.)

3. What have you learnt from the book of Ruth about God's:

   • faithfulness?

- kindness and willingness to bless?

- sovereign control of events?

Tips for leaders

Studying Ruth

The studies in *Famine and Fortune*, like all of the Interactive and Topical Bible Studies from Matthias Media, are aimed to fall somewhere between a sermon and a set of unadorned discussion questions. The idea is to provide a little more direction and information than you would normally see in a set of printed Bible studies, but to maintain an emphasis on personal investigation, thought, discovery and application. We aim to give input and help, without doing all the work for the student.

In studying the book of Ruth we confront the difficulty inherent in studying narratives in the Bible generally—that is, how to move from the story of what happened *then* to the significance for my life *now*. The story itself is not very complicated or difficult to follow. Some care, however, needs to be taken in correctly applying the truths of God's word (as we find them in Ruth) to our own situation. On the one hand, we need to avoid jumping in a simplistic fashion from the actions of the characters in the story to what we should do—such as concluding that in a time of famine or financial difficulty Christians should travel abroad (based on Ruth chapter 1). Yet, we also know that all the Bible narratives, whether in the Old or New Testaments, are God's word to us. They speak to us, providing us with encouragement, example, and hope, as the Apostle Paul says (Rom 15:4; 1 Cor 10:6-7.).

In reading an Old Testament narrative, we need to keep in mind the overall significance of the story, and its place in the story of the whole Bible, as well as noting how the narrative itself is set up.

The overall significance of Ruth for us is made clear by the verses which open and close the book. The narrative is set in the time of the judges and tells the story of how the the line of the great king-to-be, David, came to be established. It is a story of God's providential workings in the lives of ordinary people to achieve his purposes—not only in blessing them as individuals, but in advancing his historic plans for Israel as a nation and humanity as a whole. Ruth forms part of God's secret plan that was to find its fulfilment and culmination in Christ—Christ is the climactic redeemer and king, next to which all previous redeemers and kings are shadows and prefigurings.

Given this big picture of how Ruth fits into the story of the whole Bible, we can also draw lessons from the actions of the characters in the story (God being a key player of course). The narrative of Ruth is told in such a way as to invite us to notice the shortcomings of some of the characters, the strengths of others, the interaction between them, the way they relate to God, the way God relates to them, and so on.

We have tried to keep both of these things in mind as we have framed the studies.

Like all our studies, these are designed to work in a group on the assumption that the group members have worked through the material in advance. If this is not happening in your group it will obviously change the way you lead the study.

If the group is preparing ...

If all is well, and the group is well-prepared, then reading through *all* the text, and answering *all* the questions will be time consuming and probably quite boring. It is not designed to work this way in a group.

The leader needs to go through the study thoroughly in advance and work out how to lead a group discussion using the text and questions as a *basis*. You should be able to follow the order of the study through pretty much as it is written. But you will need to work out which things you are going to omit, which you are going to glide over quite quickly, and which you are going to concentrate on and perhaps add supplementary discussion questions to.

Obviously, as with all studies, this process of selection and augmentation will be based on what your *aims* are for this study for your particular group. You need to work out where you want to get to as a main emphasis or teaching point or application point at the end. The material itself will certainly head you in a particular direction, but there will usually be various emphases you can bring out, and a variety of applications to think about.

The slabs of text need to be treated as a resource for discussion, not something to be simply read out. This will mean highlighting portions to talk about, adding supplementary discussion questions and ideas to provoke discussion where you think that would be helpful for your particular group, and so on.

The same is true for the *Investigate* and *Think it through* questions. You need to be selective, according to where you want the whole thing to go. Some questions you will want to do fairly quickly or omit altogether. Others you will want to concentrate on—because they are difficult or because they are crucial or both—and in these cases you may want to add a few questions of your own if you think it would help.

You may also need to add some probing questions of your own if your group is giving too many 'pat' answers, or just reproducing the ideas in the text sections without actually grappling with the biblical text for themselves.

There is room for flexibility. Some groups, for example, read the text and do the *Investigate* questions in advance, but save the *Think it through* questions for the group discussion.

If the group isn't preparing ...

This obviously makes the whole thing a lot harder (as with any study). Most of the above still applies. But if your group is not doing much preparation, your role is even more crucial and active. You will have to be even more careful in your selection and emphasis and supplementary questions—you will have to convey the basic content, as well as develop it in the direction of personal application. Reading through the *whole* study in the group will still be hard going. In your selection, you will probably need to read more sections of text together (selecting the important bits), and will not be able to glide over comprehension questions so easily.

If the group is not preparing, it does make it harder—not impossible, but a good reason for encouraging your group to do at least some preparation.

Conclusion

No set of printed studies can guarantee a good group learning experience. No book can take the place of a well-prepared thoughtful leader who knows where he or she wants to take the group, and guides them gently along that path.

Our Bible studies aim to be a resource and handbook for that process. They will do a lot of the work for you. All the same, they need to be *used* not simply followed.

Matthias Media publishes a course in how to lead a small group. It's called *Growth Groups* and is written by Colin Marshall. For thorough training in group leadership, problem solving and goal-setting, we recommend that you work through *Growth Groups* at some stage.

Feedback on this resource

We really appreciate getting feedback about our resources—not just suggestions for how to improve them, but also positive feedback and ways they can be used. We especially love to hear that the resources may have helped someone in their Christian growth.

You can send feedback to us via the 'Feedback' menu in our online store, or write to us at PO Box 225, Kingsford NSW 2032, Australia.

Matthias Media is an evangelical publishing ministry that seeks to persuade all Christians of the truth of God's purposes in Jesus Christ as revealed in the Bible, and equip them with high-quality resources, so that by the work of the Holy Spirit they will:

- abandon their lives to the honour and service of Christ in daily holiness and decision-making
- pray constantly in Christ's name for the fruitfulness and growth of his gospel
- speak the Bible's life-changing word whenever and however they can—in the home, in the world and in the fellowship of his people.

It was in 1988 that we first started pursuing this mission, and in God's kindness we now have more than 300 different ministry resources being used all over the world. These resources range from Bible studies and books through to training courses and audio sermons.

To find out more about our large range of very useful resources, and to access samples and free downloads, visit our website:

www.matthiasmedia.com.au

How to buy our resources

1. Direct from us over the internet:
   – in the US: www.matthiasmedia.com
   – in Australia and the rest of the world: www.matthiasmedia.com.au

2. Direct from us by phone:
   – in the US: 1 866 407 4530
   – in Australia: 1800 814 360 (Sydney: 9663 1478)
   – international: +61-2-9663-1478

3. Through a range of outlets in various parts of the world. Visit **www.matthiasmedia.com.au/international.php** for details about recommended retailers in your part of the world, including www.thegoodbook.co.uk in the United Kingdom.

4. Trade enquiries can be addressed to:
   – in the US and Canada: sales@matthiasmedia.com
   – in Australia and the rest of the world: sales@matthiasmedia.com.au

Register at our website for our **free** regular email update to receive information about the latest new resources, **exclusive special offers**, and free articles to help you grow in your Christian life and ministry.

Other Interactive and Topical Bible Studies from Matthias Media:

Our Interactive Bible Studies (IBS) and Topical Bible Studies (TBS) are a valuable resource to help you keep feeding from God's word. The IBS series works through passages and books of the Bible; the TBS series pulls together the Bible's teaching on topics such as money or prayer. As at October 2009, the series contains the following titles:

BEYOND EDEN
(GENESIS 1-11)
Authors: Phillip Jensen and
Tony Payne, 9 studies

OUT OF DARKNESS
(EXODUS 1-18)
Author: Andrew Reid, 8 studies

THE SHADOW OF GLORY
(EXODUS 19-40)
Author: Andrew Reid, 7 studies

THE ONE AND ONLY
(DEUTERONOMY)
Author: Bryson Smith, 8 studies

**THE GOOD, THE BAD
AND THE UGLY**
(JUDGES)
Author: Mark Baddeley, 10 studies

FAMINE AND FORTUNE
(RUTH)
Authors: Barry Webb and
David Höhne, 4 studies

RENOVATOR'S DREAM
(NEHEMIAH)
Authors: Phil Campbell and
Greg Clarke, 7 studies

THE EYE OF THE STORM
(JOB)
Author: Bryson Smith, 6 studies

THE SEARCH FOR MEANING
(ECCLESIASTES)
Author: Tim McMahon, 9 studies

TWO CITIES
(ISAIAH)
Authors: Andrew Reid and
Karen Morris, 9 studies

KINGDOM OF DREAMS
(DANIEL)
Authors: Andrew Reid and
Karen Morris, 9 studies

BURNING DESIRE
(OBADIAH AND MALACHI)
Authors: Phillip Jensen and
Richard Pulley, 6 studies

WARNING SIGNS
(JONAH)
Author: Andrew Reid, 6 studies

ON THAT DAY
(ZECHARIAH)
Author: Tim McMahon, 8 studies

FULL OF PROMISE
(THE BIG PICTURE OF THE O.T.)
Authors: Phil Campbell
and Bryson Smith, 8 studies

THE GOOD LIVING GUIDE
(MATTHEW 5:1-12)
Authors: Phillip Jensen and
Tony Payne, 9 studies

NEWS OF THE HOUR
(MARK)
Author: Peter Bolt, 10 studies

PROCLAIMING THE RISEN LORD
(LUKE 24-ACTS 2)
Author: Peter Bolt and Tony Payne,
6 studies

MISSION UNSTOPPABLE
(ACTS)
Author: Bryson Smith, 10 studies

THE FREE GIFT OF LIFE
(ROMANS 1-5)
Author: Gordon Cheng, 8 studies

THE FREE GIFT OF SONSHIP
(ROMANS 6-11)
Author: Gordon Cheng, 8 studies

**THE FREEDOM OF CHRISTIAN
LIVING**
(ROMANS 12-16)
Author: Gordon Cheng, 7 studies

FREE FOR ALL
(GALATIANS)
Authors: Phillip Jensen
and Kel Richards, 8 studies

WALK THIS WAY
(EPHESIANS)
Author: Bryson Smith, 8 studies

PARTNERS FOR LIFE
(PHILIPPIANS)
Author: Tim Thorburn, 8 studies

THE COMPLETE CHRISTIAN
(COLOSSIANS)
Authors: Phillip Jensen and
Tony Payne, 8 studies

TO THE HOUSEHOLDER
(1 TIMOTHY)
Authors: Phillip Jensen and
Greg Clarke, 9 studies

RUN THE RACE
(2 TIMOTHY)
Author: Bryson Smith, 6 studies

THE PATH TO GODLINESS
(TITUS)
Authors: Phillip Jensen and
Tony Payne, 7 studies

FROM SHADOW TO REALITY
(HEBREWS)
Author: Joshua Ng, 10 studies

THE IMPLANTED WORD
(JAMES)
Authors: Phillip Jensen and
Kirsten Birkett, 8 studies

HOMEWARD BOUND
(1 PETER)
Authors: Phillip Jensen and
Tony Payne, 10 studies

ALL YOU NEED TO KNOW
(2 PETER)
Author: Bryson Smith, 6 studies

THE VISION STATEMENT
(REVELATION)
Author: Greg Clarke, 9 studies

BOLD I APPROACH
(PRAYER)
Author: Tony Payne, 6 studies

CASH VALUES
(MONEY)
Author: Tony Payne, 5 studies

THE BLUEPRINT
(DOCTRINE)
Authors: Phillip Jensen and
Tony Payne, 11 studies

WOMAN OF GOD
(THE BIBLE ON WOMEN)
Author: Terry Blowes, 8 studies